HOW TO USE THIS WORKBOOK

The Miracle of Life Change is more than a Bible study or small group curriculum; it is a window into the heart of God. These messages were created to help you see yourself as God sees you and inspire you to become the person you've always longed to be. These sessions will expose the lies of false expectations, explain a biblical process of experiencing lasting life change, and express the genuine expectations that God's Word provides about the nature of spiritual metamorphosis. You will find a workbook session for each video/audio presentation that includes the following helpful tools:

Video/Audio Session Notes

In each session, you'll find space for personal notes and a fill-in outline to help you follow the central points in Chip's teaching. As you watch and listen to the presentations, note the key points and Scripture passages. Take a moment after each media session to journal any personal reactions or insights. This kind of active response will help you retain the biblical lessons.

Transformation Conversation and Personal Study Notes

As you will discover, Chip emphasizes the biblical principle that genuine life change always occurs in the context of community—relationships with other believers. The questions in this section will help you prepare for and participate in your group discussion. This section also allows you to review and reflect on the content of Chip's presentation. Take some quiet time between sessions to look back at previous sessions to keep the big picture of life change fresh in your heart and mind.

P9-CAN-129

Action Steps

Using adapted quotes from Chip's teaching, these insights will help you apply the key points to your life. Take time to prayerfully consider these insights.

At Home

Each session will close with several practical suggestions for applying the biblical lessons. If you are doing this study with a group, you might consider asking others in the group to follow up with you throughout the week to see how you're doing putting these steps into practice.

Leader's Notes

We have included some brief suggestions for those using these materials in small groups and Sunday school classes. The Leader's Notes begin with some general instructions about the teaching series as a whole. Each session is then handled separately and there are some specific suggestions that will assist the leader/facilitator in planning the sessions. An answer key has been provided to help settle any confusion over the fill-in outlines. Some of the sessions will include some direction from Chip, and your preparation will enhance the learning curve of the group. The Leader's Notes will provide you with some simple but helpful guidelines along the way.

THE MIRACLE
OF LIFE CHANGE

How God Transforms His Children

Produced with the assistance of The Livingstone Corporation. Project staff includes: Mary Horner Collins, Ashley Taylor, Joel Bartlett, Linda Taylor, and Neil Wilson.

Walk Thru the Bible project staff: Dave Ball and Rebecca Gregory.

TABLE OF CONTENTS

A WORD FROM YOUR TEACHER

What is your reaction when you read this question? Do *you* believe that a changed life really can happen? If you are like most people, your gut-level, honest response is *"No."* You've tried numerous programs that promise change in various areas of life—weight, relationships, work habits, etc.—with limited if any meaningful results. You're frustrated. You may have even considered throwing in the towel and giving up on even trying to change. Let's be honest; we've all felt that hopeless at one point in time or another.

In fact, you might be struggling with an even deeper level of disappointment. You may even be thinking that Christianity has sold you a "bill of goods." For you, the Christian life may feel like a cycle of *"try hard, do good, fail; try hard, do good, fail;"* and then, when you're tired of failing, it becomes *"try hard, do good . . . fake it."* There is a growing sense of futility in your heart. The "new life" you were promised feels a lot like the "old life." And the bondage to old sinful habits doesn't seem to have been broken.

Well, I've got good news for you—there is hope! Life change is possible! But before we get started I need to warn you: **This is not a "change yourself for the better" program.** This is not a motivational plan to psych you up to try harder. I'm not here to "pump you up." I am here to share the truth and promises of God's Word and to walk beside you on your journey toward becoming the person He longs for you to be. It is a process; it is a step-by-step journey of faith. It requires focus and discipline, but in the end, you'll be equipped to experience the life God desires for you to live!

The following ten sessions will provide you with a fresh perspective on this whole idea of spiritual transformation that, I pray, will move you from the frustration of failure to the freedom you have in Christ. Join me as we discover together, *The Miracle of Life Change.*

Keep Pressin' Ahead,

President, Walk Thru the Bible

Teaching Pastor, Living on the Edge

SESSION I

IS A "CHANGED LIFE" REALLY POSSIBLE?

Butterflies don't look like caterpillars. Unless we've watched the time-consuming and agonizing process that the worm undergoes to become lighter than air, we would probably doubt anyone who told us that caterpillars become butterflies . . . unless we trusted that person. A crawler becomes a flyer? That much change sounds incredible. Almost as incredible as people changing.

Ask most people and they'll probably agree it's easier to identify with the caterpillar than the butterfly. We dream about butterfly freedom but wake up in wormy captivity. And yet, the dreams may be a hint of what we're designed to experience. What if the One who put that dream of change in you had already made it possible for your dream to become a reality?

Spiritual metamorphosis is God's will for every single believer on the planet.

God didn't create a static, impersonal universe. It resonates with divine purpose and change! As you experience these messages and work through these sessions, keep the following question in mind: If a "changed life" really *is* possible, am I willing to let God work as radically in my life as He does in a tiny caterpillar?

IS A "CHANGED LIFE" REALLY POSSIBLE?

Why do we all long to morph?

_____

_____

What is spiritual metamorphosis?

_____

_____

Spiritual metamorphosis has three stages:

1 Spiritual metamorphosis **begins** with spiritual _____.
(John 3:5-8)

Jesus becomes my Savior.

_____

_____

2 Spiritual metamorphosis **continues** toward spiritual _____.
(Ephesians 4:13; Romans 8:28-29)

Jesus becomes my Lord.

_____

_____

3 Spiritual metamorphosis **completes** its work with spiritual _____
_____. (Hebrews 5:12-14; 2 Timothy 2:2)

Jesus uses me to love others.

_____

_____

_As a prisoner for the Lord, then, I urge you to live a life worthy of the calling
you have received. Be completely humble and gentle; be patient, bearing with
one another in love. Make every effort to keep the unity of the Spirit through
the bond of peace._ —Ephesians 4:1-3 (NIV)

The Call—Let Jesus Live His Life Through You

As a prisoner for the Lord, then, I urge you to live a life worthy of the calling you have received. —Ephesians 4:1 (NIV)

Let Jesus _____ His _____ through you.

The Process—Practice Sacrificial, Other-Centered Relationships

Be completely humble and gentle; be patient, bearing with one another in love. Make every effort to keep the unity of the Spirit through the bond of peace. —Ephesians 4:2-3 (NIV)

The **first attitude**: _____

Humility begins when we decide to think of ourselves honestly and practice serving others unselfishly. (Romans 12:3; Philippians 2:3-5)

The **second attitude**: _____

Gentleness develops when we intentionally relate to people beyond our immediate comfort zone. (John 13:1-17)

The **third attitude**: _____

Patience has a chance to grow as we experience the disappointments, delays, and frustrations with those who don't want to change or don't see change the same way we do.

"Butterflies are transformed in cocoons . . . Believers are morphed in the cocoon of community."

The **fourth attitude**: _____

Bearing with one another in love takes over when we respond to apparent failure, misunderstanding, or rejection.

SESSION I *Transformation Conversation*

1 In response to Chip's closing comments, share the first time you really felt loved by God. What were the circumstances in your life when you felt His presence?

_____

_____

2 Over the next few weeks, what's the one thing you would long for God to change in your life? If you're comfortable sharing with the group, please do so and ask them to join you in prayer support.

_____

_____

3 In the "morphing" or life-change process, why do you think it is important to be in authentic community with other believers? Does your community group function at the level of authenticity Chip described? If not, why not? (If you are not currently in a group, what steps will you take to get involved regularly with other believers?)

_____

_____

4 Of the four attitudes Chip discussed (humility, gentleness, patience, bearing with one another in love), which one comes most naturally to you? Give an example. Which attitude do you need to work on the most? How will you put that attitude into practice in your life over the next week?

_____

_____

5 Describe an experience you've had in which someone really affected your life by treating you with one of the attitudes. How did that act of kindness make a difference in you?

_____

_____

THE LONGING TO MORPH is in your DNA. Intrinsic in the DNA of your soul is the desire to grow, to improve, to "change for the better." The multi-billion dollar, self-help industry has banked on our need to feel loved, desired, and accepted. Watch TV, listen to the radio, flip through a current magazine, or even drive down the street, and you'll be bombarded with advertisements that promise anything from a better memory to a better body to a better marriage—everyone wants to get better at something. Why?

What does the longing to morph look like in your life? What changes are you almost afraid of that would indicate to others that you have gone through a radical transformation? List at least three specific changes you long for God to morph in your life.

1 _____

2 _____

3 _____

GOD IS BIGGER THAN ANYTHING IN YOUR LIFE. That's the point. He wants to take your life and my life from being spiritual caterpillars and make us beautiful butterflies. He's bigger than your job, your marriage, your anxieties, your panic attacks, your fears, and your marital problems. He's *over* all, *in* all, and *through* all. He's working every day, in every way, using every circumstance, every person, and every situation, to morph you into the image of His Son. He desires to make you and me little mirrors, although imperfect, that will reflect the character, the love, the grace, and the holiness of Jesus Christ living His life through us. That's what holy transformation is all about.

In relation to each of the changes you just listed, now note which of the four attitudes in Ephesians 4:2 you would like to improve in your life so that change can begin to occur.

_____

_____

_____

THIS WEEK, take an inventory of the major changes that have occurred in your life during the last five years. Use the categorized list below to start, or use a notebook if you need more space:

General Life Changes	Spiritual Changes

FOR THE NEXT SESSION, prepare to share three areas of your life that you want to dedicate to God during your study of *The Miracle of Life Change.* Ask Him to allow you to experience some measurable, lasting change in the next several months. Make these objectives beyond what you think you can achieve by your own effort or by accident. Be willing to ask your group to pray for you as you place these personal challenges before God.

1

2

3

SESSION 2

OVERCOMING OBSTACLES TO LIFE CHANGE

L ast session we said that change is part of our DNA . . . that we are hardwired to continually "change for the better." Depending on where we are in life, we are getting faster or slower, larger or smaller, more skillful or falling behind—more changes than we can count. But if change is inevitable, then what makes it so difficult to experience the kind of **life change** we desire? Why can so many of us easily relate to Chip when he talks about the heartache and frustration of wanting to change, but feeling helpless? We all know what it feels like to try for so long to change some area of our life that sometimes we end up settling for faking it, or just plain failure. The truth is, the cycle of *"try hard, do good, fail; try hard, fail, fake it"* can be broken. You can begin to undergo the radical transformation you've been longing for—you just have to be willing to allow God access to your heart. He longs to give you the life you desire by changing you from the inside out.

In this session we begin with the underlying reason that drives spiritual transformation or life change. We have

> *"Life can't stay the same. . . . We must reflect Him living in us."*

already recognized that there is a call from God to morph—to let Jesus live His life through us. We learned that there is a process for spiritual transformation—the cocoon of authentic, godly relationships in the body of Christ. Now we will see *why* spiritual transformation is not an option for believers—it's a necessity! Then, we will step back and look at some of the primary obstacles we encounter in our journey toward spiritual transformation and explore specific ways we can overcome them.

OVERCOMING OBSTACLES TO LIFE CHANGE

The Reason—God's Church Must Reflect His Character

There is one body and one Spirit—just as you were called to one hope when you were called—one Lord, one faith, one baptism; one God and Father of all, who is over all and through all and in all. —Ephesians 4:4-6 (NIV)

_____

_____

Three primary causes lead to failure when it comes to living the transformed life:

First reason we fail to morph: Spiritual _____.

"Our failure to understand our identity in Christ and how to appropriate grace destines us to the '*try hard, do good, fail*' syndrome."

_____ _____ will never bring about the righteous life that God requires.

As a prisoner for the Lord, then, I urge you to live a life worthy of the calling you have received. —Ephesians 4:1 (NIV).

We need to understand . . .

. . . that we are justified in Christ. (Ephesians 1–3)

. . . that this growth in grace is a process. (2 Corinthians 3:18)

. . . how to appropriate the grace that's available by faith. (Romans 12:2)

The **cause** for spiritual ignorance: Lack of biblical _____.

The **cure** for spiritual ignorance: Master the English _____.

_____

_____

_____

Second reason we fail to morph: Spiritual _____.

> **"Our failure to actively participate in in-depth, Christ-centered, honest relationships makes transformation not hard, but impossible."**

_____

_____

> *"You've got to have some people that you're 'real' with . . . authentic, other-centered, vulnerable, real relationships."*

> *Be completely humble and gentle; be patient, bearing with one another in love. Make every effort to keep the unity of the Spirit through the bond of peace. —Ephesians 4:2-3 (NIV)*

The **cause** for spiritual isolation: Sin of pride.

The **cure** for spiritual isolation: Join a small group.

_____

_____

Third reason we fail to morph: Spiritual _____ (near-sightedness).

> **"Our failure to see the magnitude of 'what's at stake' in our call to Christ-like behavior minimizes its importance and shatters our motivation."**

> *There is one body and one Spirit—just as you were called to one hope when you were called—one Lord, one faith, one baptism; one God and Father of all, who is over all and through all and in all. —Ephesians 4:4-6 (NIV)*

> *"It's about Him, and His name and the integrity of His church, and a generation of people . . . I think we can start The Miracle of Life Change."*

The **cause** for spiritual myopia: We've become a _____ culture.

The **cure** for spiritual myopia: Get a high view of _____. (Isaiah 40)

_____

_____

SESSION 2 *Transformation Conversation*

1 Share what your current view of God is with the group. Where did you get your current view of God? How has it changed over the last year?
In pursuit of a more accurate view of God, what step or steps do you feel you need to take?

_____

_____

2 What's your response to Chip's question, "Have you made God a cosmic vending machine?" In what other ways has today's culture affected our view of who God is?

_____

_____

3 After hearing Chip speak about Paul's description of the church and its relationship with God in Ephesians 4:4-6, what characteristic do you long to see displayed more prominently in your church?

_____

_____

4 Are you experiencing any of the pitfalls to living a transformed life? Spiritual ignorance, isolation, or myopia? What's the cause? What's the cure? How do you plan to act on the cure this week?

_____

_____

5 Finish this sentence: My purpose on this planet is _____.
How is God using you to reflect His glory? Are you ready and willing to step outside of your comfort zone and allow Him to work in you?

_____

_____

JUST AS THERE'S MOLDING AND SHAPING THAT HAPPENS with the butterfly in the cocoon, so transformation is a process. The Bible calls this process "sanctification." A big word that basically means the moment you ask the Spirit of God to come into your life as a believer, He inhabits your heart and begins the transformation process in you.

Once you have accepted Jesus as your Savior, you have all of His Spirit that you're ever going to have. You have all the grace you'll ever need. God longs for you to progressively surrender control of who you are to Him so that the life of Christ can be lived out through you.

That's why the focus of New Testament Christianity is relationship and not works or simply morality. Do you see the difference? It's a process—a journey. Based on today's session, list what you consider to be the next two priorities God wants you to deal with in the area of spiritual transformation.

> **Priority One**
> _____
> **Priority Two**
> _____

BY AUTHENTIC COMMUNITY I'm talking about vulnerable, deep, intimate, intentionally accountable relationships where God's Word is at the center. Relationships that encourage an openness to share with one another what's really going on—confessing sin, encouraging one another, sharing where you've blown it, people looking you in the eye and saying, "I've been there too. Now you know you can't keep living that way, but I'm not down on you. I'm for you." Your group may be your family, a small group at church, or any place where genuine relationships can occur, where you feel connected and can overcome isolation.

Without this kind of authentic relationship you are destined to the "*try hard, do good, fake it*" syndrome. Millions of people are faking the Christian life, living with the guilt and struggle and lack of peace.

Identify three authentic relationships and/or community group(s) available in your life. Note one benefit each of them could offer you.

Anti–Spiritual Isolation Groups

SESSION 2 Action Steps

SESSION 2 At Home

This week, spend some time thinking and praying about Chip's closing thoughts in the video. Do you need to repent about the casual way you have been thinking about God? Have you had to admit that the struggle to describe your view of God is because you haven't thought about Him very much? Remember that Chip's purpose wasn't to make you feel guilty, but to help you simply clear away some of the obvious self-centered misconceptions of God. God loves you and longs for a personal relationship with you. Open your heart and mind and ask God to use these sessions to help you gain a significantly higher view of who He really is.

What are some of the words you've heard used to describe God (like holy, sovereign, loving, omnipresent) that you want to understand better so that you can better understand the One they describe? Make a personal list in your journal and begin to develop definitions.

For the next session, carefully read Ephesians 4:1-10, reflecting on the contents of the last two sessions. Answer the question: What was Jesus doing from the time He was put into the grave until He rose three days later?

If you are already part of a small group, take some time to pray specifically for each of the members this week.

SESSION 3

HOW DO YOU DEAL WITH THE PROBLEM OF SIN?

L et's let the cat out of the bag and talk frankly about the biggest challenge that keeps us from continually experiencing the miracle of life change. The answer is pretty simple—it's **sin**! What keeps us from becoming like Jesus is **sin**! When our flesh is in control, we're not experiencing the holy transformation God intended for us. Instead of letting the Holy Spirit be in control and help us live out our new identity in Christ, we've allowed our flesh to be controlled by the impulses of **sin**. So the real question in life change turns out to be, **How do we deal with the problem of sin?**

In this session, Chip will walk us through some unfamiliar territory to discover a wonderful insight that will give us the foundation of hope for meaningful life change. These verses include some vivid imagery that would have been immediately familiar to Paul's first readers, but may have been glossed over the last time you read Ephesians 4:7-10.

> *"Let's let the cat out of the bag and talk frankly about the biggest challenge that keeps us from continually experiencing the miracle of life change. The answer is pretty simple—it's sin!"*

As Chip begins to unpack these verses, listen carefully. These verses contain a compelling message of hope. They have the power to change our whole way of thinking. They describe an amazing scene we need to understand if we're going to get serious about genuine spiritual transformation.

HOW DO YOU DEAL WITH THE PROBLEM OF SIN?

But thanks be to God that though you were slaves of sin, you became obedient from the heart to that form of teaching to which you were committed, and having been freed from sin, you became slaves of righteousness.
—Romans 6:17-18 (NASB)

But now that you have been set free from sin and have become slaves to God, the benefit you reap leads to holiness, and the result is eternal life.
—Romans 6:22 (NIV)

There are three key phrases in Ephesians 4:7-10:

But to each one of us grace was given according to the measure of Christ's gift. Therefore it says,

> *"When He ascended on high,*
> ***He led captive a host of captives,***
> *and He gave gifts to men."*

*(Now this expression, "He ascended," what does it mean except that He also had descended into **the lower parts of the earth?** He who descended is Himself also He who ascended far above all the heavens, **so that He might fill all things).** —Ephesians 4:7-10 (NASB)*

First key phrase: He led captive a _____ of captives.

Psalm 68:18 makes the point that the gifts given out of the spoils of war reminded the people of the king's generosity and the great victory achieved against the enemy. Likewise, out of His love for us and His victory on the cross, Jesus gives us spiritual gifts as a daily reminder of His defeat of Satan.

Second key phrase: The _____ parts of the earth.

The Jewish people in Jesus' time pictured death divided into two compartments (see, for example, Luke 16:19-31). One was the destination of the unrighteous dead and the other held the righteous dead: Hades and Paradise.

Hades: *For Christ died for sins once for all, the righteous for the unrighteous, to bring you to God. He was put to death in the body but made alive by the Spirit, through whom also he went and preached to the spirits in prison. —1 Peter 3:18-19 (NIV)*

Paradise: *For this is the reason the gospel was preached even to those who are now dead, so that they might be judged according to men in regard to the body, but live according to God in regard to the spirit. —1 Peter 4:6 (NIV)*

Third key phrase: That He might _____ all things.

And they sang a new song:

> *"You are worthy to take the scroll and to open its seals,*
> *because you were slain,*
> *and with your blood you purchased men for God*
> *from every tribe and language and people and nation.*
> > *You have made them to be a*
> > *kingdom and priests to serve our God,*
> > *and they will reign on the earth."*
> > > *Then I looked and heard the voice of many angels,*
> > > *numbering thousands upon thousands,*
> > > *and ten thousand times ten thousand.*
> > > *They encircled the throne and the living creatures and*
> > > > *the elders.*

In a loud voice they sang:

> *"Worthy is the Lamb, who was slain,*
> *to receive power and wealth and wisdom and strength*
> *and honor and glory and praise!"*

Then I heard every creature in heaven and on earth and under the earth and on the sea, and all that is in them, singing:

> *"To him who sits on the throne and to the Lamb*
> *be praise and honor and glory and power,*
> *for ever and ever!" —Revelation 5:9-13 (NIV)*

> *"What keeps us from becoming more like Jesus is sin."*

Every believer of every age gets _____ exactly the same way, by grace through faith.

SESSION 3 Transformation Conversation

1 In what ways do you identify with the young man and woman who approached Chip, both reading verses from Romans 6 about freedom from sin and then stated, "It's not working for me"? After listening to this session, what would you have said to them?

_____

_____

2 *But thanks be to God that though you were slaves of sin, you became obedient from the heart to that form of teaching to which you were committed, and having been freed from sin, you became slaves of righteousness. —Romans 6:17-18 (NASB)* Where are you acting as a slave to sin in your life? What power do you have over this sin now that you realize you are freed from sin and are now a slave to righteousness?

_____

_____

3 How would you describe your approach to dealing with the problem of sin up to this point in your life? How has this teaching changed your view of sin?

_____

_____

4 What "spoils" of war or spiritual gifts has God given you? How are you using them in your life today? If you don't think you have any gifts, are you willing to ask God to show you?

_____

_____

5 Why is it crucial to understand that our relationship with Christ rests on what is true, not what we feel at any particular moment?

_____

_____

_____

SESSION 3 *Action Steps*

SIN AND DEATH ARE TWO WEAPONS Satan continually uses to intimidate, frustrate, and prevent us from pursuing life change. He reminds us of past sins and exploits our weaknesses and tendencies toward sin. Unfortunately, we tend to give him plenty of ammunition to use against us because we do sin. But the facts behind the verses we've studied in this lesson remind us that Satan can make loud noises, but he's shooting blanks. Our sins can't be used against us once we've let Christ take care of them, and death no longer threatens us as it did before Christ's work on the cross. Romans 8:1 tells us, "Therefore, there is now no condemnation for those who are in Christ Jesus," (NIV) which means that the sting and power of death have been nullified by Christ's death and resurrection.

The triumph Jesus achieved by beating Satan at his own game and disarming the power of sin and death outshines any achievement in history. It has a greater effect on our lives than any other experience. Based on this session, list what you see as the most precious spiritual gifts Christ has given you as a result of His victory over sin, death, and Satan.

Gifts from Christ's great victory

_____

_____

_____

AS BELIEVERS WHO'VE BEEN FORGIVEN, we don't have to fear death, but can actually look beyond it with anticipation. Without Christ, death is a frightening stronghold that threatens to swallow us. Death is the fortress we can't defeat, and the enemy king is Satan. The good news in these verses is that the fortress has been overrun and ransacked. Jesus won the victory. In Christ we have something beyond and far above death to look forward to enjoying.

God's Word gives us many startling pictures of the atmosphere of heaven. Revelation 5:9-13 gives us a picture of the greatest worship service ever, and if you have trusted Christ, you will be part of that countless choir. Take a moment now and imagine singing those words to Jesus. Write down what it will mean for you to offer "praise, honor, glory, and power" to Christ. You might find it helpful to think of your favorite praise song or hymn for inspiration.

I will praise Jesus by _____.

I will honor Jesus by _____.

I will give glory to Jesus by _____.

I will recognize Jesus' power by _____.

THIS WEEK, make it a point to rest on Christ's work. Consider inviting one or more friends to meet with you for the purpose of praise. Ask each of them to think of a song or two that helps them appreciate Christ and allow them to share their reasons when you gather. Enjoy a personal praise concert together.

FOR THE NEXT SESSION, read Ephesians 4:7-10 again and picture as vividly as you can the scene of Jesus marching in triumph having achieved the greatest victory. Allow the truth to sink into your soul that because He has done all the impossible work, you get to enjoy the benefits forever. Let those thoughts motivate some personal times of gratitude and praise between you and God.

Ask God for the wisdom to remember what Christ has done for you when you are tempted to rely on your fleeting feelings or present circumstances to judge your position in Christ.

SESSION 4

WHERE DO WE GET THE POWER TO CHANGE?

Have you ever sat back and imagined exactly what the battle between Christ and Satan might have looked like? If you had been there as an observer, what would you have done? How would you have felt? In the last session we looked at a passage of Scripture we might normally be tempted to gloss over. However, upon closer examination, we discovered these verses give a powerful picture of the work Christ accomplished for us!

Christ's victory over sin, death, and Satan far outshines any other event in history. But, beyond the good feelings that victory gives us, what else does it mean? Given the reality that we face opportunities to sin every day, how does Christ's presence in our lives affect our hope of defeating old habits, conquering temptation, and living the life we've always longed to live?

In this session we will see how Christ's victory can be ours. The same power that Jesus exercised in conquering sin, death, and Satan is

> *"Christ's victory over sin, death, and Satan far outshines any other event in history."*

available to us! The answer to our deepest longing for change is found in the resources that are ours in Christ.

WHERE DO WE GET THE POWER TO CHANGE?

The Implications of Christ's Victory for Spiritual Transformation

Fact #1: Christ is a _____ victor over sin, death, and Satan. The power to live a new life was made possible by His death and resurrection. (Romans 6:1-4)

The personal results of Christ's work on the cross mean:

1 You are _____. (Romans 6:17-18)

2 You have power over death; therefore, you are _____. (Romans 6:22-23)

3 You are _____. (Colossians 2:13-15)

Principle #1 The miracle of life change always begins with the _____ . (John 8:32; 17:17)

_____

_____

A mind and a heart _____ with God's Word is the prerequisite for life change.

_____

_____

Fact #2: We become "_____" of Christ's victory over sin, death, and Satan the moment we receive Christ as our personal Savior by faith. (Ephesians 2:1-8)

_____

_____

Principle #2 Life change demands that we _____ on the truth.
(John 8:31)

_____ is believing God to the point of acting on what He
said whether you feel like it or not.

_____

_____

Fact #3: Every believer is given a _____ _____
(a supernatural enabling) at the moment of salvation for two reasons:

　　1. To remind us that life change occurs on the basis of grace, not

　　_____-_____.

　　2. To remind us that we have a special, supernatural empowerment that
　　makes us _____-_____ "agents of grace" who
　　supply what others need to morph into the likeness of Christ.

Principle #3 Life change is both a gift and a responsibility.

_____

_____

SESSION 4 *Transformation Conversation*

1 What does it mean to you to be called a "co-partaker" of Christ's death as well as of His victory over sin, death, and Satan?

_____

_____

2 How does the biblical picture of Jesus as the conquering victor over sin, death, and Satan affect your hope of personal life change?

_____

_____

3 Do you live as though you have power over sin? Why or why not? What is one temptation you are struggling with that you're willing to share with the group and ask for prayer about?

_____

_____

4 What did you find helpful in Chip's illustration of the block of wood, the knife, and the tape to show the way Christ, a person, and faith function in harmony?

_____

_____

5 Since life change demands both initial and ongoing acts in response to the truth, how would you describe the crucial moment when you first acted on God's offer of salvation? What are some of the ongoing faith actions that characterize your life?

_____

_____

SESSION 4 Action Steps

APPLIED IMPLICATIONS

THE IMPLICATIONS OF CHRIST'S VICTORY lead directly to certain life-changing applications. Let's take, for example, the way in which the three principles in this lesson affect our thinking. For each of the principles listed below, provide one answer to the attached question:

Principle #1: **The miracle of life change always begins with the truth.**

What are you doing to get God's truth in your life? _____

Principle #2: **Life change demands that we act on the truth.**

What specific action step have you taken in the last seven days where God has shown you a truth? _____

Principle #3: **Life change is both a gift and a responsibility.**

What do you plan to do in the next few days that will demonstrate that you understand both the "gift" part and the "responsibility" part of all that Christ has done for you? _____

CHIP HAS INTRODUCED the parallel ideas of co-death and co-resurrection with Christ as crucial aspects of our spiritual lives (Romans 6:4). "As a result of what Christ has done for us," he says, "we don't have to sin. We still can sin and we still do sin, but we don't *have* to sin. We have been given Christ's authority to exercise power over sin. The only power sin has in our lives is the power we give to it." In preparation for experiencing life change, take a few moments to note below some places in your life where you know you are allowing sin to have power over you. Make that list a matter of prayer starting now and through the sessions to come. Refer to the list from time to time throughout this Bible study and see how your understanding of the principles of life change deepens.

SIN'S STRONGHOLDS WITHOUT LEGITIMATE AUTHORITY.

I WANT TO AFFIRM CHRIST'S OWNERSHIP AND AUTHORITY IN THE FOLLOWING AREAS OF MY LIFE THAT OCCUPIED BY SIN.

_____

_____

_____

_____

SESSION 4 At Home

THIS WEEK, think about Chip's closing example of handling the worry of major decisions. Choose an area that has been challenging to you and identify a verse from Scripture that allows you to "turn that issue over to God." Write the problem on one side of a card and the verse on the other. Use that card as a reminder to pray throughout the week—make the verse yours and let God have the problem. The more of these areas you bring into the open and turn over to God, the more likely you are to experience authentic change in your life.

FOR THE NEXT SESSION, read Ephesians 4:11-16 and think about the ways other Christians have made a positive impact on your life over the years. What believers have been your up close and personal heroes in the faith—not necessarily famous, but effective in your life? If most of the people you know were doing this same assignment, how many would put you on their list of people who have had a positive spiritual influence in their lives?

In response to this session, pray that the participants in this study will respond with honesty and courage to the Holy Spirit's prompting in exposing areas of their lives that have been under the control of sin.

SESSION 5

THE BODY OF CHRIST

HOW GOD BRINGS OUT THE BEST IN HIS CHILDREN

C an you imagine becoming the kind of person you've always longed to be? God's Word provides a game plan for you to become like Jesus. Think of someone you really respect. What characteristics does that person have that draw you to spend time with him or her? God intends to do something very personal and special as He transforms each of us into the likeness of His Son. That's why He didn't give us all the same gifts or abilities. He wants our service to one another to be meaningful—we actually need each other! Just as the cells in the human body have basic components but specific duties and abilities, so it is in the body of Christ. We all share certain character traits and needs, but our Creator has intended each of us for very special service that the rest of the body requires.

The person we long to be will emerge from a process God has designed. We examined the call to morph and the process of morphing (Ephesians 4:1-2) in the first session.

> *"The person we long to be will emerge from a process God has designed."*

Now we will look at how transformation occurs. In addition to the attitudes of humility, gentleness, patience, and bearing with others in love that develop through our relationships with other Christians, Paul now describes certain unique gifts that God equips some in the body to use for the specific training of others. No believer is exempt from this training process.

HOW GOD BRINGS OUT THE BEST IN HIS CHILDREN

What is God's game plan for transforming His children?

And He gave

> *some as apostles,*
> *and some as prophets,*
> *and some as evangelists,*
> *and some as pastors and teachers,*
> *for the equipping of the saints for the work of service,*
> *to the building up of the body of Christ;*
> *until we all attain*
>> *to the unity of the faith,*
>> *and of the knowledge of the Son of God,*
>> *to a mature man,*
>> *to the measure of the stature which belongs to the fullness of Christ.*

As a result,

> *we are no longer to be children,*
>> *tossed here and there by waves,*
>> *and carried about by every wind of doctrine,*
>>> *by the trickery of men,*
>>> *by craftiness in deceitful scheming;*
> *but speaking the truth in love,*
> *we are to grow up in all aspects into Him*
> *who is the head, even Christ,*
> *from whom the whole body,*
>> *being fitted and held together by what every joint supplies,*
>> *according to the proper working of each individual part,*
>> *causes the growth of the body for the building up of itself in love.*
>> *—Ephesians 4:11-16 (NASB)*

> "The person we long to be will emerge from a process God has designed."

How God Brings Out the Best in His People— The Church

Leaders are gifted to _____ God's people for service. (Ephesians 4:11-12a)

_____

_____

Apostles—those who break through, start new things, pioneer.

_____

_____

Prophets—those who take the Word of God in a culturally relevant way and deliver it to others.

_____

_____

Evangelists—those who are gifted to share the gospel in such a way that people come to Christ and motivate others to share their faith.

> *"A pastor's job is not to shepherd all the people; a pastor's job is to make sure all the people get shepherded."*

Pastors/Teachers—those who shepherd, comfort, and help others to grow in their relationship with Christ.

_____

_____

Every member is a _____.
(Ephesians 4:12)

_____

_____

> *"God's game plan is multiplication—massive impact—not for a few hired professionals to do the work."*

God has called _____ to be a minister of the gospel of Jesus Christ.

_____

_____

SESSION 5 *Transformation Conversation*

1 How are you actively equipping people in your circle of influence? List the names of those you're equipping and pray for them this week.

_____

_____

2 Where are you currently ministering in the body of Christ? Share an area of personal ministry involvement. How has your involvement impacted your personal spiritual growth? Why?

_____

_____

3 Why is it so crucial that members in the body of Christ understand that they are called and gifted, and that they need to be equipped to be the real "ministers" in the church?

_____

_____

4 In what ways did you relate to Chip's stories about people holding on to the concept of the pastor as the one who meets everyone's needs instead of the biblical model of equipping leadership? Would you describe your church as ministry by too few or ministry by many?

_____

_____

5 Do you currently have a mentor, leader, or coach? If so, what characteristics are you learning from that person's model? If not, what will you do to identify someone with those gifts?

_____

_____

SESSION 5 *Action Steps*

THIS SESSION BEGAN with a look into the future. Not an easy-going future, but a future of significant challenges and deep satisfaction flowing from spiritual maturity. Christ has empowered His church to be the place where people grow up spiritually. He has gifted certain people within His body to be His tools for equipping other believers for service. According to Jesus, everyone in the body serves everyone else. You may start out thinking you have nothing to offer other believers, but God called you into His body as a cell, an intimate component, connected by Christ with other believers. God has entrusted you with gifts that can help others.

Think about those who are serving spiritually in your life right now. What people has God provided in your church, small group, or class who are serving in the equipping roles that you need? Begin to identify the gifts of others around you. Ask God to give you insight. When you notice someone exercising a gift, let that person know. Often, people are unaware of the positive effect they are having for Christ. Use the grid below to begin identifying those people.

	Biblical Leadership Roles	Potential Equippers I Know	What I've Noticed about Them
Apostles			
Prophets			
Evangelists			
Pastors/Teachers			

GREAT ENERGY FLOWS FROM KNOWING that we belong and that we have a purpose. The personality traits we desire to exercise ultimately have little to do with titles or labels. We long to leave an impact for good on those around us. That longing may be distorted and covered by many conflicting priorities, sins, and hurts in life, but it remains. We want our lives to mean something. We were created with divine design and purpose.

In the action step above, we focused on those serving and equipping *into* our lives. In this action step, we want to track how service flows *out* of our lives. Think about both the services you are presently performing and opportunities that may be open to you. Use the grid below to list at least two of each, but expand the grid in your journal or a notebook and begin to compile a portfolio to help you identify your gift(s). This exercise will help you prepare for the next session.

	Service	Am Doing/Could Do	Gift Indication
Present Service			
Present Service			
Opportunity			
Opportunity			

SESSION 5 *At Home*

THIS WEEK, say "Thanks" to at least one person (an equipper) who has been a positive role model in your life. Be specific in your description of how that person has helped you be a better servant of Christ. By the way, if this comes easy to you, you may have the gift of encouragement, but all of us are commanded to encourage those around us. You can do this by writing a letter of appreciation to the person, emailing, calling, or even taking them out for coffee and telling them in person. The choice is up to you!

FOR THE NEXT SESSION, carefully read Ephesians 4:11-16 as you ponder an important question: How will you measure or know when life change is occurring in you?

Pray for the leaders and equippers in your life by name.

SESSION 6

HOW TO BECOME THE PERSON YOU'VE ALWAYS LONGED TO BE

How do you know you're making progress in the transformation process? That you're becoming the person you've always longed to become? Do you have to wait until you "get there" to actually see results, or are there signs you can watch for along the way? What are the clues or hints that tell us our spiritual transformation is underway and that we are growing in maturity?

In this session we will look closely at what it means to develop spiritual maturity. There are character traits and choices that you will find in the life of someone who is making significant progress toward life change. You will see that there are four evidences that accompany spiritual metamorphosis, and that those are the building blocks to spiritual maturity. These evidences will also show us some of the reasons behind our lack of significant transformation. If we are neglecting one or more of these evidences, we will prevent ourselves from experiencing the miracle of life change. Fortunately, there are some specific steps we can take to include these actions and attitudes in our daily lives.

> *"If we are neglecting one or more of these evidences, we will be preventing ourselves from experiencing the miracle of life change."*

As part of this session, Chip has created a special "diagnostic checkup" tool that will help you gauge areas in your life where life change is occurring. The "checkup" will also give you some insight on where you may choose to make some personal adjustments toward your goals for transformation.

HOW TO BECOME THE PERSON YOU'VE ALWAYS LONGED TO BE

Ministries are developed to help believers to live every day in every way just as Jesus would if He were living out His life in their _____.

> Until we all attain to the unity of the faith, and of the knowledge of the Son of God, to a mature man, to the measure of the stature which belongs to the fullness of Christ. —Ephesians 4:13 (NASB)

Ministries need to be birthed out of people's _____ and relationships.

_____

_____

Spiritual Maturity

How does a person know if he or she is spiritually mature? God measures spiritual maturity by specific, fourfold criteria:

> As a result, we are no longer to be children, tossed here and there by waves and carried about by every wind of doctrine, by the trickery of men, by craftiness in deceitful scheming. —Ephesians 4:14 (NASB)

The first evidence of spiritual maturity is _____ _____.

_____

_____

> But speaking the truth in love, we are to grow up in all aspects into Him who is the head, even Christ . . . —Ephesians 4:15 (NASB)

The second evidence of spiritual maturity is _____ _____.

_____

_____

> . . . From whom the whole body, being fitted and held together by what every joint supplies, according to the proper working of each individual part . . . —Ephesians 4:16a (NASB)

The third evidence of spiritual maturity is _____ _____ in the body of Christ.

_____

_____

. . . Causes the growth of the body for the building up of itself in love.
—*Ephesians 4:16b* (NASB)

The fourth evidence of spiritual maturity is that you _____ ___ _____.

Are you positioned where life change can happen to you?

_____

_____

A Diagnostic Checkup

1 I am currently being equipped for ministry by:

- ❑ Worshiping regularly
- ❑ Meeting regularly with an evangelist or shepherd leader
- ❑ Listening to teaching tapes
- ❑ Being involved in an apprenticeship and/or mentoring relationship

2 I am currently ministering and building into the lives of others:

- ❑ Rarely or sporadically
- ❑ Functioning in my gifts with joy and fruitfulness
- ❑ But I don't feel deeply useful
- ❑ Regularly seeing other's lives changed through me and my gifts

3 I am becoming more like Christ in my everyday life as evidenced by:

- ❑ A desire to read God's Word
- ❑ A disciplined study and understanding of God's Word
- ❑ An ability to "see through" false teaching

4 I am becoming more like Christ in my everyday life as evidenced by:

- ❑ Enjoying one or more deep, authentic relationships in Christ
- ❑ My regular attendance in a small group where "speaking the truth in love" is common
- ❑ Having three or four gut-level accountability relationships that are helping me through the most sensitive areas of my life

5 I am also becoming more like Christ in my everyday life as evidenced by:

- ❑ A desire to become more deeply involved with God's people (worship, classes, friendships)
- ❑ A sense of belonging and acceptance in my church body
- ❑ A clear sense that I "fit" in this body (I am loved by others and find myself caring for and helping them in increasing measure)

SESSION 6 *Transformation Conversation*

1 After reviewing your Diagnostic Checkup, where and how are you being equipped for ministry? What opportunities for equipping are available to you right now?

_____

_____

2 Forget for a moment about fears, the past, and other limitations. Think about your spiritual gifts and talents. What type of ministry have you always dreamed of being a part?

_____

_____

3 Are you currently positioned to build into the lives of others? In what ways?

_____

_____

4 Where do you struggle most in your pursuit of becoming more like Christ in your everyday life?

_____

_____

5 Complete each of the following sentences as brief definitions of the four spiritual maturity criteria that Chip explained in this session:

I will develop **doctrinal stability** as I . . .

_____

I will develop **authentic relationships** as I . . .

_____

I will come closer to **full participation** as I . . .

_____

I will develop **growing love** as I . . .

_____

THE DIAGNOSTIC CHECKUP you just filled out is meant to encourage you not only by showing you how far you've come in spiritual growth, but also by giving you an awareness of where there may be areas for growth. Remember, life change isn't about trying harder, so this tool isn't intended to spur you into a frenzy of activity. In fact, as you will see in later sessions, this tool can help you see where you need to go into training.

For now, review the diagnostic tool and highlight those one or two areas in which you are making progress. Refer to these as you thank God for the work He is doing in your life. Stay the course in those areas. Also, note one or two places you checked that could be handled not with more *effort*, but with *exposure*. For example, under entry 1, if you checked none of the boxes, then maybe you have not been exposed to some of the tools God often uses to inform and direct spiritual transformation. Why not ask your study group for some help in finding new resources for plugging into some good spiritual outlets?

Evidences of Growth	Exposure Decisions

DOCTRINAL STABILITY, authentic relationships, full participation, and growing capacity are four key evidences of spiritual maturity. You will learn to spot and encourage these in your own life, if you take the time to watch for them in your life and in the lives of others. The point is not to judge or be critical of others, but to look for positive traits in their lives that you want to see in your own. It will probably involve asking them how God brought about these healthy practices in their life.

Use the following grid to make some notes of significant examples of the four evidences of maturity. Think about the spiritually influential people in your life. Review the definitions Chip gave for each evidence. Try to put at least one name in each category. Once you've filled in the grid, make it a point to contact each of those people and thank each one for the example he or she has been to you. Consider asking what practices or experiences God used to build that kind of maturity in their lives.

Doctrinal Stability	Authentic Relationships	Full Participation	Growing Capacity

SESSION 6 *At Home*

THIS WEEK, put into action at least one "Exposure Decision" you made as part of the first action step above. Also, contact at least two of the people whose example you noted in the spiritual maturity grid.

FOR THE NEXT SESSION, mentally step back and reflect on what you've learned to this point in these sessions. How are you thinking about life change and spiritual transformation in different ways than you have before? What changes are you actually seeing in yourself?

Use Philippians 1:6 as a prayer for yourself and the others who are in the remainder of these sessions with you: *Being confident of this, that he who began a good work in you will carry it on to completion until the day of Christ Jesus. (NIV)*

SESSION 7

HOW TO "BREAK OUT" OF A DESTRUCTIVE LIFESTYLE

Remember the time-lapse photography clip in the first session that showed a butterfly emerging from a cocoon? Let's have an instant replay. Imagine that you've turned on the sound and widened the lens to show that there are two butterflies emerging side by side. You get to eavesdrop on their first conversation as they prepare to take flight. Their escape from the cocoons gets them out of a tight spot and into a major decision: turn back or continue the process.

Now, you get to decide which one of those butterflies will represent your life. It's time for you to decide how to "break out" of the destructive lifestyle that is keeping you from living the changed life you already possess.

> *"It's time for you to decide how to 'break out' of the destructive lifestyle that is keeping you from living the changed life you already possess."*

In this session we begin to deal with the leftover baggage and habits that we bring with us into our new lives as Christians. As long as we insist on keeping and carrying these things from our old lives around with us, we can't "take flight." We're like freshly hatched butterflies who refuse to leave their cocoons behind. We may look like flyers, but we act like crawlers. That's why Chip says, "A believer whose life does not change is an oxymoron." We will find that God loves us too much to leave us in that condition. He has provided a way out. We can do more than emerge from the cocoon; we can leave it behind. We can break out of a destructive lifestyle.

HOW TO "BREAK OUT" OF A DESTRUCTIVE LIFESTYLE

A Tale of Two Butterflies

Barbara's answer to the wonderful possibilities beyond the precarious perch outside the cocoon on the branch is to *take off*!

Benny's answer to the wonderful possibilities beyond the precarious perch outside the cocoon on the branch is to *return to the cocoon*!

A New Life demands a *new lifestyle*!

> If anyone is in Christ, he is a new creation; the old has gone, the new has come! —2 Corinthians 5:17 (NIV)

Which butterfly most represents you?

_____

_____

Warning: Two Common Errors to Avoid

1 _____—turns the Christian life from a supernatural relationship into laws, duties, and rules.

2 _____—turns the Christian life from a supernatural relationship into "anti" (meaning "against") and "nomianism" (meaning "the law"). This means no rules, no discipline, all grace.

_____

_____

"A believer whose life does not change is an _____**!"**

Look at Ephesians 4:17-24 (NIV, emphasis added) as we unpack the message:

> So I tell you this, and insist on it in the Lord, that you must no longer live as
> the Gentiles do, in the futility of their thinking.
>> They are <u>darkened</u> in their understanding and <u>separated</u> from the life of God
>> because of the <u>ignorance</u> that is in them due to the <u>hardening</u> of their hearts.
>> Having lost all <u>sensitivity</u>, they have given themselves over to <u>sensuality</u>
>> so as to indulge in every kind of <u>impurity</u>, with a continual <u>lust</u> for more.
>
> <u>You</u>, however, did not come to know Christ that way.
> Surely you <u>heard</u> of him and were <u>taught</u> in him in accordance with the <u>truth</u>
> that is in Jesus.
> You were taught, with regard to your former way of life,
>> to <u>put off</u> your old self, which is being corrupted by its deceitful desires;
>> to <u>be made new</u> in the attitude of your minds;
>> and to <u>put on</u> the new self, created to be like God in true righteousness and
>> holiness.

As believers, our lives must be progressively characterized by _____

_____. (Ephesians 4:17-19)

_____

_____

An immoral lifestyle is _____ for us as believers
for two reasons:

1 It contradicts _____ we are!
(Ephesians 4:20)

2 It contradicts _____ Christ is!
(Ephesians 4:21)

_____

_____

SESSION 7 *Transformation Conversation*

1 How would you describe the time of silence and prayer, followed by confession, that we just experienced? In what ways was it like Benny and Barbara's moment of "teetering on the branch" between take-off or retreat for you?

_____

_____

2 Chip has just emphasized that there is a real tension between the familiar old life and the central issue of genuine freedom from sin in a Christian's new life. In what ways have you experienced this tension?

_____

_____

3 Is your life constantly changing, or are you stuck holding onto old baggage? What is keeping you from letting go? What makes it difficult to lay down the old you at the foot of the cross and live in the freedom of Christ?

_____

_____

4 Why do you think the Apostle Paul presented such a vivid picture of life outside of Christ in Ephesians 4:17-19, even though he was writing to believers? How did this explanation help you understand God's desire for you to live your life as a new creation in Christ?

_____

_____

5 If our lives as believers must be progressively characterized by moral purity, then how do the two false versions of purity below (moralism and antinomianism) contrast with the third—the biblical definition of purity? Which false version do you struggle with and why?

a. **Moralism:** Moral purity earns God's favor.

b. **Antinomianism:** Moral purity is irrelevant because grace super-abounds when I sin.

c. **Biblical definition**: Moral purity is the natural outgrowth of who I am as a child of God; it reflects His character and holiness.

_____

_____

SESSION 7 Action Steps

LIFE OUTSIDE THE COCOON IS SCARY to those familiar with the old life. For Benny, the fear associated with the unknown world held him captive in the familiarity of his cocoon. Instead of trusting his wings, he chose to reenter the cocoon he no longer fit. He became stuck between two worlds. As Chip has said, "The most miserable person is the butterfly trying to live as a worm."

But Barbara left the cocoon behind in every way. Her attention was so focused on the new life and all its possibilities that she didn't even miss the old. For her, the excitement of finding out what it meant to be a "new creation" held all her attention. Once she began to experience that reality, she couldn't imagine going back.

Given that all believers carry in them both Benny and Barbara tendencies, list personal examples from each area in your life.

Benny's Bad Habits to Leave Behind	Barbara's Beneficial Attitudes to Develop

TAKE A MOMENT TO DESCRIBE BELOW the inward struggle you experienced during the time of silence at the end of the video session. What emotions did you feel? Fear, excitement, adventure, exhilaration, doubt, sadness? Were the choices you made about what to share based more on what you thought was acceptable or on what God's Spirit was pointing out to you?

_____

_____

_____

_____

THIS WEEK, make it a point to observe others who are "in flight." Their lives won't be perfect, but rather than focus on their failures or flaws, notice what God is doing in and through them. Let them know what you see. It will be a powerful encouragement. In doing so, you will be putting into action some of the earlier lessons about the role of others in your own life change.

FOR THE NEXT SESSION, read Ephesians 4:17-20, reflecting on the contents of the past sessions. Jot down a few ideas that Paul seems to be repeating for emphasis as he continues to spur the Ephesians toward life change.

Ask God for a healthy dose of "holy recklessness" as you dream about stepping off branches and flying boldly where you haven't dared to fly before.

SESSION 8

GOD'S THREEFOLD PRINCIPLE OF TRANSFORMATION

In our last session, we looked at the empty and decayed cocoons of our old lives and talked about having "been there, done that," and not ever wanting to go there again (as tempting as it might be to do so at times). Having received the light of Jesus in our lives, we have a built-in dislike about our former lives in darkness. To live as we formerly did no longer makes sense. A believer whose life does not change has an oxymoronic life—trying to get back into a lifestyle where he or she no longer fits.

In this session, we turn from the practical comparisons of our old life to the challenges of the new life we've been given in Christ. God's Word spells out a process that allows us to shed the residue of the old, experience deep transformation from within, and then replace the old with something new and vibrant. The change isn't instant, but it's real. We may long for quick results, but God has a better plan. He wants to bring about lasting, authentic life change in us. His principles will allow us to break free from our old habits and the destructive choices we used to make and live the life of freedom He designed.

> *"We may long for instant results, but God has a better plan. He wants to bring about lasting, authentic life change in us."*

GOD'S THREEFOLD PRINCIPLE OF TRANSFORMATION

You were taught, with regard to your former way of life, to put off your old self, which is being corrupted by its deceitful desires; to be made new in the attitude of your minds; and to put on the new self, created to be like God in true righteousness and holiness. —Ephesians 4:22-24 (NIV)

We achieve personal purity by following God's threefold principles of trans-formation or life change.

_____

_____

Principle #1: _____ _____ (point in time) the old!
(Ephesians 4:22)

_____

_____

Three destructive behaviors that are common and "culturally acceptable" in America are:

Materialism—believing that how much I accumulate will make me feel good and acceptable.

People-pleasing—believing I can't say "no," and continually feeling the unacceptability threatening me and reminding me that I'm not OK. I can't bear to disappoint anyone.

Workaholism—deep insecurities that cause me to believe that enough achievement will make me feel good and acceptable. I'm driven.

> *"God's relationship with you is 100 percent unconditional love all the time, regardless of your performance."*

What destructive behavior patterns do you need to "put off"?

_____

_____

_____

Principle #2: _____ _____ (continuously) in the spirit of your mind! (Ephesians 4:23)

> *I urge you, brothers, in view of God's mercy, to offer your bodies as living sacrifices, holy and pleasing to God—this is your spiritual act of worship. Do not conform any longer to the pattern of this world, but be transformed by the renewing of your mind. Then you will be able to test and approve what God's will is—his good, pleasing and perfect will. —Romans 12:1-2 (NIV)*

_____

_____

You get your mind renewed and your _____ changes.

> *"I am accepted in the Beloved, I am secure in Him, I have all that I need from You."*

_____

_____

Principle #3: _____ _____ (point in time) the new! (Ephesians 4:24)

_____

_____

> *"The most important decision you make every single day is not what food you put in your mouth. The most important decision that will impact you, your marriage, your children, your grandchildren, your life, your future, your legacy— the most important decision every day is what you put in your mind."*

1 Based on Chip's closing challenge, what things, habits, behavior, or attitudes are you considering "putting off"? What decisions do you need to make?

_____

_____

2 Write a brief explanation of your understanding of each of the threefold principles of transformation that Chip introduced in this session.

"Put off" means . . .

_____

"Be renewed" means . . .

_____

"Put on" means . . .

_____

3 When Chip speaks openly about the struggles of workaholism, people-pleasing, and materialism, what are the "put off, renew, put on" principles he is putting into practice?

_____

_____

4 Did you relate personally to any of the struggles Chip shared above? If not, identify one personal struggle that you would like to "put off." What next steps will you take to renew your mind and "put on" God's best for your life?

_____

_____

5 What would be the most noticeable change in your daily pattern if you took Chip up on his challenge to take a media fast—a break from the usual routine?

_____

_____

SESSION 8 *Transformation Conversation*

YOU CAN SLIP INTO SIN, but you've got to break through to holiness. Chip has just pointed out that life change begins with definitive action. What do you need to put off? For some of us, the main action in "putting off" involves a decision. It may boil down to deciding we can't go to the bars and hang out with our buddies anymore. This is not a rejection of people but a new understanding that we simply can't handle certain situations in a healthy way. If we hang out in the bars until one or two in the morning, our Christian life looks more like the old life than the changed life.

Most of us can readily think of areas in our lives that God has been pointing out that need to be "put off." We don't need to try to figure out if it's a problem anymore. We need to make a decision. We need to make a conscience choice—to choose His ways above our own.

What behaviors has God been impressing on you that you know you need to "put off" by starting this threefold process related to that area? Write today's date beside each item you list. Ask for help in filling out the "mind renewal verse" and "put on" columns.

Things I've been putting off putting off

Put Off	Mind Renewal Verse	Put On

HAVE YOUR MIND RENEWED. Romans 12:2 insists that we not be conformed to this world but, instead, have our minds renewed. Ephesians 4:23 makes the same point. That's why God's Word is so important. God longs to help you. He is eager for a real, personal, and authentic relationship with you, but He can't do it without your participation in getting to know Him through His Word.

Identify an area where you struggle in life. Then discover the promises in God's Word that apply to that struggle. You may have to ask help to fill in the center column above. Read those promises, write them down, and commit them to memory. Allow God to speak to you in that area of your life. Define the lie that Satan has deceived you with and renew your mind with the truth God has given you in His Word. Over time this renewal will gradually change the way you respond to the "triggers" that disrupt your life. Over time, little by little, you will experience freedom that a life in Christ has to offer—you will experience genuine life change. Use the sample below to begin a "mind renewing" card system in your life.

Based on Your promise recorded on the reverse of this card, I will . . .

SESSION 8 *At Home*

THIS WEEK, why not take Chip up on a personal experiment with a "media fast"? Here's how you can occupy your newly found spare time. Use some Bible study tools, or ask someone more knowledgeable to help you find promises and passages from God's Word that speak to the behaviors in your life you have decided to put off. Let God renew your mind as you focus on His Word. Write out the kinds of cards Chip described in this session with a description of one of the old lifestyle attitudes on one side and a promise from God on the other. Review those cards daily in thought and prayer.

FOR THE NEXT SESSION, read Ephesians 4:24-32, noting character words that could represent articles of clothing you would like to put on your life.

Set aside a half hour to meditate on the meaning of three words: *Relationship with Christ*. Ask God to help you sense the wonder of that privilege. Ask Him to teach you to avoid reducing that relationship to habits and actions that you do without thinking or feeling. There's no one He wants to spend time with more than you.

SESSION 9

RYAN'S STORY

THE ROLE OF SPIRITUAL TRAINING IN THE LIFE-CHANGE PROCESS (PART 1)

How does this work? Butterflies, birds, and angels have actual wings—we don't. So, how do we go beyond the inspiration of metamorphosis in nature to the miracle of life change in our very real and sometimes frustrating situations? How do we unleash the power of Jesus' victory over sin, death, and Satan in our lives so that transformation occurs? How do we turn our cocoons inside out so that all the shameful, harmful, persistent sins are exposed to the truth? Most of us confess that we have tried, sometimes very hard, to deal with these matters. And we have failed. What does God have to tell us about life change?

Beginning with this session, we will "go into training" and examine five major areas of our lives where lasting life change can occur. But, before we can start applying these training

> *"Most of us confess that we have tried, sometimes very hard, to deal with these matters. And we have failed. What does God have to tell us about life change?"*

stations, we'll examine the testimony of Chip's son, Ryan, who struggled with a very basic besetting sin—an area of his life that continued to trouble him. Ryan wanted very badly to overcome his sin, but he soon realized he couldn't do so by "trying harder." The issue boiled down to a core character trait. The solution Ryan discovered will work for you too, if you are willing to "go into training"!

SESSION 9 Notes

THE ROLE OF SPIRITUAL TRAINING IN THE LIFE-CHANGE PROCESS (PART 1)

Review of Sessions 1 and 2

Ryan knew that every believer is _____ to morph or change. (Ephesians 4:1-6)

_____

_____

Review of Sessions 3 and 4

Ryan knew that Christ's defeat of _____, death, and Satan makes morphing or life change possible. (Ephesians 4:7-10)

_____

_____

Review of Sessions 5 and 6

Ryan knew that the church is God's _____ _____ of transformation or morphing in our lives. (Ephesians 4:11-16)

_____

_____

Review of Sessions 7 and 8

Ryan also knew that we achieve _____ _____ by God's threefold principle of transformation. (Ephesians 4:17-24)

1 Put off

2 Be renewed

3 Put on

_____

_____

SESSION 9 *Notes*

What Ryan had to learn: Transformation is a matter of spiritual _____ versus trying harder. (Ephesians 4:25-32)

_____

_____

Spiritual Training Station #1: Personal Integrity—Honesty

Be _____. Speak the truth in love.

But speaking the truth in love, we are to grow up in all aspects into Him who is the head, even Christ. —Ephesians 4:15 (NASB)

Therefore, laying aside falsehood, speak the truth each one of you with his neighbor, for we are members of one another. —Ephesians 4:25 (NASB)

_____

_____

Training Objective: _____. (Personal Integrity)

Training Command: "Speak the _____ in _____."

Training Actions:

Put Off—Falsehood

_____

_____

Renew—Recognition of _____ membership in the body

_____

_____

Put On—Speak the _____.

_____

_____

SESSION 9 *Notes*

Be honest or have integrity in the _____ _____.
(Luke 16:10)

_____

_____

The **Training Apparatus:** Practice _____.

Spiritual Training Station #2: Emotional Control

Be _____. Deal with anger appropriately.

> *Be angry, and yet do not sin; do not let the sun go down on your anger, and do not give the devil an opportunity.* —Ephesians 4:26-27 (NASB)

_____

_____

Training Objective: Emotional _____.

Training Command: Be angry, but do not _____. (Ephesians 4:26-27)

> *Let the peace of Christ rule in your hearts, to which indeed you were called in one body; and be thankful. (Colossians 3:15 NASB)*

Training Actions:

Put Off—Anger that leads to sin and

_____.

_____

Renew—Recognize that _____ and unrighteous anger is the _____ in which demonic activity enters your heart and your mind.

_____

_____

Put On—Appropriate expressions of _____.

_____

_____

Training Apparatus: Use "____ _____" messages.
(Romans 12:17-21)

> *What would happen in your relationships if you began to use "I feel" messages?*

Do not repay anyone evil for evil. Be careful to do what is right in the eyes of everybody. If it is possible, as far as it depends on you, live at peace with everyone. Do not take revenge, my friends, but leave room for God's wrath, for it is written: "It is mine to avenge; I will repay," says the Lord. On the contrary: "If your enemy is hungry, feed him; if he is thirsty, give him something to drink. In doing this, you will heap burning coals on his head." Do not be overcome by evil, but overcome evil with good.
—Romans 12:17-21 (NIV)

_____

_____

_____

Emotional Control
Ephesians 4:26-27

_____

Personal Integrity — Honesty
Ephesians 4:24-25

_____

SESSION 9 *Notes*

SESSION 9 *Transformation Conversation*

1 As you listened to the group respond to Chip's instructions about sharing areas of life in need of spiritual training, what other issues came to mind that you know will require you to go into spiritual training if you want to experience the miracle of life change?

---

2 How have you experienced the difference between "trying hard" and "training"? In what ways did you relate with Ryan's frustrations over trying hard and failing repeatedly?

---

3 Notice that the Training Pyramid still has three more levels to be introduced. Why do you think integrity serves as the foundation for this five-station training sequence in the process of life change? What does the term *integrity* mean to you?

---

4 What was a significant example of truthful speech that someone practiced with you? How did it impact your life?

---

5 To what degree has anger against self, others, and God been an issue in your life? What do you think would happen in your relationships if you began to regularly use "I feel" messages?

TRYING IS AN "ALL OR NOTHING" APPROACH with no other response to failure than to admit defeat. For *trying*, failure is the enemy that usually wins. For *training*, failure simply factors into the process. For *training*, failure is actually a sign that some progress has been made, even if only a little. *Trying* almost assumes defeat, while *training* works toward an objective, going over, under, around, and through failures. *Trying* begins with high immediate expectations, few strategies, and low long-term expectations. *Training* begins with low immediate expectations, clear strategy, and high long-term expectations. *Training* often succeeds where *trying* frequently fails.

List some nagging issues in your life and begin to plan strategically about an incremental training approach to them. Even before submitting them to the training process you've begun to learn in this session, think about the objective you want to accomplish. Choose at least one area that you can visualize improvement in, and describe clearly what that improvement would be. Put a time frame on the high expectation. The outline below will help you handle at least one area.

Life Area	Present Unsatisfactory Condition	Reasonable Training Time Frame	Expected Results

THE PRINCIPLES OF WEIGHT LIFTING rely on the amazing capacity human muscles have for getting stronger, not the idea that exercise creates new muscles. Different kinds of demands create different kinds of responses in muscles. Some training regimens increase a muscle's flexibility and endurance, while other exercises increase power. As you think through the content of these sessions so far and the principles of life change that Paul included in Ephesians 4, begin to develop a list of the "muscles" or resources you have because you are a new creation in Christ. While you didn't get wings when you trusted Christ, you did receive other priceless gifts that can be exercised and will become stronger, more effective, and more flexible. As a new creation in Christ, you have more potential than you can imagine. Your list of personal spiritual resources will come in handy as you move into training.

Gifts, Resources, and Capacities I Have in Christ

_____

_____

_____

_____

THE BACKLOG OF DISHONESTY may be overwhelming. You may even hesitate about starting spiritual training in this area because the list of places in your life that lack integrity seems too long. Remember, it's like a barbell with too much weight. You will not be able to lift it all. You will need God's help even in knowing where to start. But you do need to start.

Begin by making a list of relationships and instances (like work or home) where your pattern has been lack of integrity. Keep that list with your Bible and cross off each item as you deal with it. Ask God to help you begin to "practice confession" in some of these relationships in order to whittle down the backlog. Also undertake your training in integrity today by prayerfully signing the integrity code below.

When God's Spirit convicts me of a dishonest word or action,
I will practice confession and make it right.

Signed: _____. *Date:* _____.

ANGER ISN'T JUST blowing off steam or repressing emotion—absolutely not. Unresolved anger makes you and me vulnerable to spiritual attack. I believe this passage lets us know why demonic activity occurs among God's people. Anger gives Satan a foothold to exploit. He gets a free ticket to create chaos. Unresolved anger between a husband and wife can be ignored, but it's still there and it leaks poison into their souls and their marriage. Appropriate expressions of anger are the answer. But how do we carry out the command in Ephesians 4:26 to be angry, yet not sin?

In order to put into practice the training apparatus that will strengthen our emotional control, we need to think of a long-standing habit by our spouse that really bothers us. Instead of exploding, retaliating, or repressing, we should start using "I feel" messages.

In order to do this, you will need to identify the wound that is coming out in anger. How *does* his or her action make you feel? Use the following tool as a sample to begin working on handling anger.

Repeated Aggravating Action	How It Makes Me Feel	How I Will Share These Feelings

SESSION 9 *At Home*

THIS WEEK, spend some time each day reflecting prayerfully on your identity in Christ. Keep referring to your Gifts, Resources, and Capacities list from the Action Steps. As God expands your awareness of the nature of your new life, add to that list. Refer to it when you are developing a strategy to respond to ongoing struggles or emerging challenges in your life.

Also, meditate on the trait of integrity. Consider that it isn't a claim or aim not to do anything wrong, but the serious effort to correct things when you do them wrong. Integrity not only acknowledges imperfection; it treats dishonesty with confession and (if necessary) restitution. The person of integrity knows how to say, "I was wrong. Will you forgive me?" Integrity is the core of personal responsibility. A helpful Scripture passage is Matthew 5:1-11, where the Beatitudes describe the behavior of a person of integrity.

FOR THE NEXT SESSION, read Ephesians 4:25-32, this time underlining or noting particular areas where God is speaking to you about your life.

Ask God for a genuine willingness to enter training in areas that may have become entrenched places of defeat and shame in your life. You may not yet be able to visualize victory, but acknowledge that God is more eager to help with your weaknesses and failures than you can imagine. Ask God for a renewed sense of personal integrity as you allow Him to bring about the miracle of life change in you.

SESSION 10

THE ROLE OF SPIRITUAL TRAINING IN THE LIFE-CHANGE PROCESS (PART 2)

Remember in the last session, when Ryan felt the weight of "trying hard" firsthand? He grew tired and frustrated when change didn't occur overnight. As you may already have discovered from your own failed attempts, the principles we've been talking about don't happen immediately. They are developed when you decide to go into training. Your first efforts may be awkward. That's why we're taking these last two sessions and breaking each component down into easily identifiable steps: the training objective, command, actions, and apparatus. Over time, you will begin to see the results of Christ living His life through you.

As you go into training, remember to take small steps. Building your muscles takes perseverance. If life's challenges feel like they're weighing heavy on you, don't get discouraged. Put the load down for a moment and take a deep breath and rest. That's what training is all about—learning to lift a little more each day; over time your spiritual muscles will grow. Keep in mind, you are not lifting the weight alone. Start by asking God to give you the strength. Transformation will follow.

> "You have to go into training. Your first efforts may be awkward . . . Over time, you will begin to see the results of Christ living His life through you."

As we wrap up our time together, I want to encourage you—you can become the person you've longed to become. Follow God's game plan outlined in His Word. The results will be worth it! The same power that resurrected Jesus and defeated sin, death, and Satan lives inside you. The Holy Spirit gives you the ability to fight sin, live a godly life, and morph into the person God wants you to be! The miracle of life change can happen to you!

SESSION 10 *Notes*

THE ROLE OF SPIRITUAL TRAINING IN THE LIFE-CHANGE PROCESS (PART 2)

Spiritual Training Station #3: Financial Stewardship

Be _____. Work hard and refuse to take "shortcuts."

> *He who steals must steal no longer; but rather he must labor, performing with his own hands what is good, so that he will have something to share with one who has need.* —*Ephesians 4:28 (NASB)*

_____

_____

Training Objective: _____ _____. (Work Ethic)

_____

_____

Training Command: "_____ no longer." Ephesians 4:28

Training Actions:

Put Off—Stealing.

_____

_____

Renew—Think differently about the _____ of work.

_____

_____

Put On—Work.

_____

_____

I need to develop a stewardship mentality versus a shortcut mentality.

> *Whatever you do, do your work heartily, as for the Lord rather than for men, knowing that from the Lord you will receive the reward of the inheritance.* —*Colossians 3:23-24a (NASB)*

Training Apparatus: _____ _____.

_____

_____

Spiritual Training Station #4: Speech Patterns

Be _____. Don't wound with your words.

> *Let no unwholesome word proceed from your mouth, but only such a word as is good for edification according to the need of the moment, so that it will give grace to those who hear. Do not grieve the Holy Spirit of God, by whom you were sealed for the day of redemption. —Ephesians 4:29-30 (NASB)*

_____

Training Objective: Positive _____.

_____

Training Command: "Say only what _____." (Ephesians 4:29)

Training Actions:

Put Off—Any _____ word.

_____

Renew—Give grace to others and avoid grieving the Holy Spirit.

_____

Put On—_____, encouraging speech.

There is _____ and death in the _____ of words. (Proverbs 10:11)

Words reveal your _____. (Luke 6:45)

There is a reality of _____. (Matthew 12:36)

_____

_____

SESSION 10 Notes

But I tell you that every careless word that people speak, they shall give an accounting for it in the day of judgment. —Matthew 12:36 (NASB)

Training Apparatus: Practicing _____ and _____.

_____

_____

Let there be no more foul language, but good words instead—words suitable for the occasion, which God can use to help other people.—Ephesians 4:29 (Phillips)

Spiritual Training Station #5: Private Attitudes

Be _____. Be the first to say, "I'm sorry."

Let all bitterness and wrath and anger and clamor and slander be put away from you, along with all malice. Be kind to one another, tender-hearted, forgiving each other, just as God in Christ also has forgiven you. —Ephesians 4:31-32 (NASB)

_____

Training Objective: _____ speech.

_____

_____

Training Command: "Be _____ to one another, tender-hearted, forgiving each other." (Ephesians 4:32a NASB)

Training Actions:

Put Off—_____

_____

_____

Renew—New _____ based on what God has done for you.

_____

_____

Put On—_____.

Training Apparatus: Matthew 5:24 principle:

In every relationship that is not right, YOU take the initiative.

Therefore if you are presenting your offering at the altar, and there remember that your brother has something against you, leave your offering there before the altar and go; first be reconciled to your brother, and then come and present your offering. —Matthew 5:23-24 (NASB)

Private Attitudes
Ephesians 4:31-32

Speech Patterns
Ephesians 4:29-30

Financial Stewardship
Ephesians 4:28

Emotional Control
Ephesians 4:26-27

Personal Integrity — Honesty
Ephesians 4:24-25

SESSION 10 Transformation Conversation

1 Of the five basic spiritual training stations—Personal Integrity, Emotional Control, Financial Stewardship, Positive Speech, and Private Attitudes— which one would you consider your area of greatest personal maturity at the moment?

2 Which station do you recognize as the most pressing area (that besetting sin Chip mentions) in which you need to go into spiritual training? When and how do you plan to begin?

3 Describe the level of accountability you have in life at the present time. Who could be that accountability partner for you that Chip mentioned in his closing?

4 In what situations or relationships do you find the greatest need for increasing your capacity for positive speech? Describe a time when some-one else's use of positive speech made a huge impact on your life.

5 Respond to Chip's final challenge: What's all this going to look like in your life three or four months from now? What will it take to make that happen?

SESSION 10 Action Steps

WHAT IF YOU DECIDED TO LIVE OFF A "TO BE" LIST rather than a "to do" list? "To dos" are constant, and we rarely get our lists done. If we put off our "to be" priorities until after we've done our "to dos," we'll never "become." What would happen if you put a "to be" list together and scheduled the activities you know will contribute to those objectives first in your day-timer or calendar? What if you translated what you say is really important into specific time slots on your schedule that you honor like all other appointments?

Think of the examples Chip used from his daily routine and marriage, and begin to compile a list of the "to be" qualities that you want to characterize your life. Start with a simple objective like: "I will deliberately schedule at least one 'to be' item on my schedule every day." Fill in the sample below to help picture what that might look like.

JANUARY 1

TO DO:

_____

_____

_____

_____

TO BE:

_____

_____

DON'T LET STUFF COME OUT OF YOUR MOUTH THAT MAKES GOD SAD.
The way we speak and act toward our brothers and sisters in Christ (and even those not yet in Christ) communicates to God how we feel about Him. John makes it clear that we can't say we love God and yet hate our brother (1 John 4:20). James points out that the control of the tongue is like control of the rudder that guides the entire ship (James 3:4-5). What we say reflects who we are. This training station and the next demonstrate the progressive aspects of God's plan—things get harder because we're dealing with the central matters of the heart. This doesn't mean we try harder; it means we trust God and stay in training.

SESSION 10 *Action Steps*

Getting on the apparatus of silence and solitude requires a deliberate choice. Silence and solitude won't show up unless they are invited. They may even have to be captured, because moments of quiet are so fleeting in our hectic world. A few moments each day, an hour a week, a half a day each month—these are worthwhile time goals. We need to stop talking long enough to think clearly about what we have been saying! Use Chip's card system to record untruths and then write God's response or truth on the opposite side. That way you can begin practicing positive speech.

(Front)	(Back)
I'm lying when I see a need I can meet but excuse my lack of involvement.	"But whoever has the world's goods, and sees his brother in need and closes his heart against him, how does the love of God abide in him?" (1 John 3:17 NASB)

OUR STARTING POINT FOR FORGIVING others rests in a deep understanding and overwhelming gratitude for Christ's forgiveness. It is the huge standard we must remember. "Bearing with one another, and forgiving each other, whoever has a complaint against anyone; just as the Lord forgave you, so also should you" (Colossians 3:13 NASB). Once we develop some skills and habits in the discipline of silence and solitude, we can begin to ponder the wonder of Christ's forgiveness. The more we experience the depth of God's grace and mercy, the more we will be ready to forgive others.

The apparatus here starts us out, not with forgiving others but with the Matthew 5:23-24 rule of asking others to forgive us or making things right with someone who "has something against us." Dedicate some time in the next day or so to pondering any nagging sense of uneasiness or brokenness in your relationships. Use the space below or your journal to list and strategize how and when you will approach those people to seek reconciliation.

Because Christ went the distance to be reconciled with me, I will take steps to be reconciled with . . .

_____

_____

_____

_____

THIS WEEK, deliberately use at least one "I feel" message in a conversation with someone you love. As Chip illustrated, if you have a pattern of other responses, you will get an almost immediate sense that something is different. Also, take a look at your calendar/PDA and begin to think about scheduling specific "to be" appointments. Remember Chip's caution that the last two training stations are Ph.D. level cardio/spiritual workouts. Spend some of your time reflecting on and praying about your starting place rather than how far you have to travel. As Chip illustrated from his own life, the process of life change lasts a whole lifetime.

SINCE THIS IS THE LAST SESSION, make sure you have some kind of action plan in place. Write down an appointment for six months from now to review this workbook and measure your progress. In the meantime, focus on training rather than trying harder. Keep the increments small and doable even if they don't appear all that significant at the moment.

Ask God for one or two ongoing relationships in the body of Christ who will commit with you to a life of spiritual training and mutual accountability. Now, spread those butterfly wings and fly!

SESSION 10 At Home

THE MIRACLE OF LIFE CHANGE

Welcome to this audio/video study of a crucial aspect of the Christian life. If you are facilitating a group's experience of these teaching sessions, we want to encourage and help you as much as possible. The idea of leading others in a study can be uncomfortable and terrifying, but we're convinced that you've already taken the biggest step if you have made yourself available for God to use in this way.

Preliminary: Because *The Miracle of Life Change* involves a teaching journey, it's important for the group to start together. You may want to schedule an introductory session in which you pass out the workbooks, "introduce" Chip to the group, let participants meet each other, and start to get a sense of the personalities in the group.

Extras: Make sure you have enough workbooks. For those in the group who are readers, consider having several copies of the book Chip has written that has the same title as the audio/video series.

Remember:

You get to prepare. Take advantage of the opportunity. The more you think and pray about the content of the session ahead of time, the more relaxed you will be as a facilitator.

Suggested Basic Approach: R.E.A.D.Y.

Review the session materials, including the video. Outline how you will approach each session.

Engage in prayer for the group time and the individual participants.

Ask others to help in aspects of the sessions, like running the video equipment, welcoming others, sharing experiences.

Dedicate each session to the Lord, asking Him to continue to work out His miracle of life change in you and the others in the group.

You're ready.

Leader's Notes

YOU CAN CLAIM IGNORANCE, even if you think you know the answer. Be prepared to say, "I don't know." That will encourage the whole group to think seriously. Invite others to answer questions ("Would anyone else like to take a crack at this one?"). Unanswered questions often drive us to seek God. Make a note of loose ends and seek further input from God's Word and the counsel of other Christians.

Check your Checklist:

⮑ Time/Location confirmation. Aim at a 60-minute session but have 90 minutes available if at all possible.

⮑ DVD/VHS player and large enough monitor.

⮑ Operator of equipment.

⮑ Session helps—any props you decide to use.

⮑ Session materials, spare pens, extra workbooks, your Bible!

SESSION 1: IS A "CHANGED LIFE" REALLY POSSIBLE?

Introduction and Video Notes

⤣ If you haven't had an earlier Introductory session, take a few minutes to make sure people know one another's names.

⤣ Lead the group through the first pages of the workbook, pointing out the "How to Use This Workbook" page and encouraging people to review those basic instructions.

⤣ Remind people that the video notes are provided so they can experience the teaching while keeping track of the main points in Chip's presentation.

⤣ As one way to "introduce" Chip to the group, consider reading the "Word from Your Teacher" page. It will help prepare the group for Chip's style and theme.

⤣ When you turn to the first page in Session 1, encourage the group to make it a habit to read the opening thoughts before they come to a session each week. It will help them "warm up" for the challenging thoughts Chip will present.

⤣ Before starting the video for the first time, ask if there are any questions. Giving people permission to ask can set the group at ease.

Fill-In Observations

⤣ Most of the Scripture passages that Chip "unpacks" in this study have been printed in the workbook. Encourage group members to keep their Bibles open to Ephesians 4 as a "default setting" during the sessions for easy reference.

⤣ Sometimes, particularly with new Christians, it's helpful to point out what the little (NASB, NIV) letters mean after Scripture verses. In this case they represent the New American Standard Bible and the New International Version. Those are the two primary versions Chip will use in this series.

Fill-In Answer Key

1. birth

2. maturity

3. reproduction

4. live, life

5. Humility

6. Gentleness

7. Patience

8. Bearing with one another

Transformation Conversation

🖎 Encourage the group to turn to the "Transformation Conversation" page.

🖎 Remind them that there will probably not be time each session to discuss all the questions. They can use the questions for their own further study and to review in preparation for the next session.

🖎 Give them permission to "pass" on any question, but encourage them to participate in the discussions.

🖎 Choose the two or three questions that you feel most significant to discuss as a group.

🖎 Keep an eye on the clock. It's better to stop a conversation while it is "hot" than to keep going beyond the agreed time. Unfinished discussion can continue after those who must leave have been released. Exhausting conversations can keep people from returning.

Action Steps

🖎 Depending on the intensity and length of the Transformation Conversation, you may have time for one or both of the Action Steps.

🖎 Ask someone to read the quote from Chip to the group then give the group a minute or two of silence to work on their personal answers.

🖎 Again, time may be a factor, but give the group an open invitation to share what they plan to do in their Action Steps.

At Home

🖎 As you close the meeting, be sure to thank the group, for their participation.

🖎 Pray (or ask someone to pray) for the coming study and focus on thanksgiving for the miracle of life change.

🖎 Remind everyone that there are some homework assignments to prepare for the next session.

SESSION 2: OVERCOMING OBSTACLES TO LIFE CHANGE

Introduction and Video Notes

⁀ Welcome everyone back.

⁀ Give people a chance to raise questions from the last session or clarify things they heard. Use the rest of the group to help in this process.

⁀ Open with a brief prayer.

⁀ Refer to the second part of the At Home assignment and give any who would be willing the chance to share briefly an area in which they are longing to see some measurable change or growth in the next several months.

⁀ Thank those who share and start the video.

Fill-In Observations

⁀ Take a moment at the end of the video presentation to make sure people aren't frustrated with blanks.

Fill-In Answer Key

1. ignorance
2. Self-effort
3. knowledge
4. Bible

5. isolation
6. myopia
7. consumer
8. God

Transformation Conversation

⁀ Before getting into specific questions, ask the group for personal observations about the teaching session.

⁀ Choose two or three questions that you feel most significant to discuss with the group.

Action Steps

⁀ Read or have someone in the group read each of the quotes from the two action steps. Give the group time to reflect and write their answers.

⁀ Open discussion for any sharing or observations.

At Home

🔶 Encourage the group to work on the first At Home assignment throughout the week.

🔶 Point out to them that the second assignment may involve them in thinking about something they have never wondered about before.

🔶 Close in prayer.

SESSION 3: HOW DO YOU DEAL WITH THE PROBLEM OF SIN?

Introduction and Video Notes

🔶 Welcome the group and open with prayer, asking God for special ability to concentrate and follow challenging biblical ideas and concepts.

🔶 Ask everyone to open their Bibles to Ephesians 4:7-10. Depending on your group and their level of exposure to Scripture, you might want to read the verses aloud for familiarity, assuring them they will hear them again soon.

🔶 Point out that the lengthy quote from the book of Revelation that Chip uses at the end of the session is printed in the workbook.

🔶 Start the video teaching.

Fill-In Observations

🔶 Pause after the video to make sure everyone has been able to fill in their blanks.

Fill-In Answer Key

1. host

2. lower

3. fill

4. saved

Transformation Conversation

↪ Begin with question 1 and work your way down as time allows. Encourage people to note their own answers even if they don't feel free to share or you run out of time.

Action Steps

↪ Give the group a few minutes to read and respond to the two Action Step exercises silently.

↪ The sharing from the second exercise should naturally move the group toward a corporate closing prayer time. Encourage all to participate in some way to verbalize the way they think they might finish those sentences.

At Home

↪ Before you dismiss the group, remind them that this session has been a heavy teaching session and that much of the application Chip will give them has been saved for the next time. That's why the home assignments are relaxed. They're supposed to practice "resting in Christ."

SESSION 4: WHERE DO WE GET THE POWER TO CHANGE?

Introduction and Video Notes

↪ Welcome and opening prayer.

↪ Consider reading the opening introduction (or ask a group member ahead of time to read it). It will capture some of the tension left over from the last session and prepare the group for the practical aspects of this one.

↪ Start the video.

Fill-In Observations

↪ Now that you're four sessions into the study, observe who's keeping up with the fill-ins and who may not be that involved. They might just be concentrating on listening, but they may also be confused or troubled. If you note anyone like that, consider giving them a personal call between sessions to talk about how they are feeling about the study.

Leader's Notes

Fill-In Answer Key

1. conquering

2. free

3. forgiven

4. secure

5. truth

6. saturated

7. co-partakers

8. act

9. faith

10. spiritual gift

11. self-effort

12. other-centered

Transformation Conversation

☞ Pick two or three questions, discussing as long as time allows.

☞ If the group is getting quite comfortable, ask them if there are other questions they have from this session or even previous ones. You may not have time to address them in this session, but make a note of them. During your preparation for the next session, glance at the sessions to come to see if it appears Chip answers those particular questions later. Or build time for discussion of those questions into the next session.

Action Steps

☞ The second Action Step is a private exercise, so you will need to focus on the first step. Read each Principle statement and then give the group some time to work on completing the commitment phrase before discussing the issues involved.

At Home

☞ Bring index cards or some other kind of cards with you to the meeting and pass them out so that members can prepare the cards for posting at home.

☞ Point out the other parts of the assignment and assure them that you really appreciate their prayers.

☞ Close in a prayer that affirms Jesus as the ultimate source of power to change.

SESSION 5: HOW GOD BRINGS OUT THE BEST IN HIS CHILDREN

Introduction and Video Notes

↩ Welcome the group and open with prayer.

↩ Acknowledge that this session is the midway point in the study.

↩ Take a moment to let people reflect on what they have learned up to this point.

↩ Chip will begin his session with an "imagine" exercise, so move right into the video by pointing out that the lengthy passage on the next page will be the source of Chip's teaching.

Fill-In Observations

↩ Check the fill-ins for frustrating blanks.

Fill-In Answer Key

1. equip

2. minister

3. you

Transformation Conversation

↩ The questions in this session are exploratory. You should be able to move through them in order.

↩ Be alert to any tendency on the part of the group to drift into a lot of blaming or fault finding with the church. Remind them that we're not called to be critics but to be contributing members of the body ourselves. If God has promised to provide what we need for spiritual growth, we need to trust His power to provide and emphasize cooperation in the body of Christ over criticism of others.

Action Steps

↩ These two action steps deserve a significant amount of group discussion. In some groups, the capacity for the other members in the group to help identify gifts and talents may come into play. Encourage that role within the group.

At Home

↩ Note the assignment before you close in prayer.

Leader's Notes

SESSION 6: HOW TO BECOME THE PERSON YOU'VE ALWAYS LONGED TO BE

Introduction and Video Notes

↦ Welcome and prayer.

↦ Ask if anyone has an experience to share related to their assignment to express gratitude to someone who has equipped them in some aspect of the faith.

↦ Alert them that Chip will be using a diagnostic tool during the session and that there is a copy in their workbook for them to use during that exercise.

↦ Start the video.

Fill-In Observations

↦ They should be pros at this by now.

Fill-In Answer Key

1. body

2. giftedness

3. doctrinal stability

4. authentic relationships

5. full participation

6. grow in love

Transformation Conversation

↦ Have some fun with question two.

↦ Review the other questions to decide in what order to approach them and how many to cover.

Action Steps

↦ Give the group several minutes to work on the two Action Step exercises. There may be some practical or logistical questions that come out of the group during this time.

↦ As you prepare to close in prayer, consider asking the members to share at least one item from their plans for implementing the insights they got from the diagnostic checkup so that you can all be praying for each other in this process of life change.

At Home

Before you dismiss the group, remind them to take some time to review the home assignment.

Ask them to read the brief introduction to the next session before they arrive.

SESSION 7: HOW TO "BREAK OUT" OF A DESTRUCTIVE LIFESTYLE

Introduction and Video Notes

Welcome and prayer.

Chip does a great job setting up this session with the story of Benny and Barbara. You can move quickly to the video unless there are "house-keeping" duties to do.

Start the video.

Fill-In Observations

Observe how the members in the group respond to Chip's story. Their body language may give you some clues to the struggles some of them are having that they may not have been able to verbalize during the discussions.

Fill-In Answer Key

1. Moralism

2. Antinomianism

3. oxymoron

4. moral purity

5. inconceivable

6. who

7. who

Transformation Conversation

Choose two or three questions from the teaching, and work through them as time allows, unless your preview and awareness of issues in your group leads you in another direction.

Action Steps

✒ As you turn to this section, remind the group that they may want to return to these Action Steps as part of their assignment for the week, but that you'd be interested in hearing any immediate responses they have to the two exercises.

At Home

✒ In your closing prayer you might mention your hope that the members of your group will experience some of the joys of stepping off their branches and out of their comfort zones in the next week.

SESSION 8: GOD'S THREEFOLD PRINCIPLE OF TRANSFORMATION

Introduction and Video Notes

✒ You might start with a greeting like, "Well, for all of us who have been busy doing our best impression of Barbara flying off the branch this week, thank you for coming in for a landing in this session! Before we pray, does anyone have a flight adventure they would be willing to share with us?"

✒ Pray for the group, focusing on the important principles of life change that will be the focus of the last three sessions. Ask God to make each person receptive to His particular plan for his or her life.

Fill-In Observations

✒ These are simple but crucial. Make sure each group participant has placed the right term in the correct blank. You can do this by simply reviewing the answers before moving into the Transformation Conversation.

Fill-In Answer Key

1. Put off

2. Be renewed

3. thinking

4. Put on

Transformation Conversation

☞ Acknowledge that there is a growing personal tone to many of these questions and that you appreciate the vulnerability and honesty you've seen and heard in the group. Tell them it's a indication to you that they are already experiencing some of the insights Chip will share in the last sessions.

☞ The progression of these questions is straightforward. Use as many as you have time to cover. If you haven't done so before now, ask different people to "ask the question" and admit that one of the nice things about being the "asker of the question" is that it gets you off the hot seat of having to be the "answerer of the question."

Action Steps

☞ Read or have someone read each of the two Action Step exercises. After each one, give the group a few minutes to reflect and then encourage sharing of their decisions.

At Home

☞ Alert the group that this week's assignment involves multiple days. Encourage them to start within twenty-four hours.

☞ Announce that in some ways all the teaching up to this point has been laying a foundation for the next two sessions. Tell them they are about to discover some very practical insights for spiritual development.

☞ Close in prayer, acknowledging the "never-ending" process of growth in spiritual maturity while we remain on this side of eternity.

SESSION 9: THE ROLE OF SPIRITUAL TRAINING IN THE LIFE-CHANGE PROCESS (1)

Introduction and Video Notes

☞ Welcome and prayer.

☞ The video session will be longer this time, so make sure to keep things moving.

Leader's Notes

↪ Alert the group to the fact that Chip will begin with a review of the central points he's covered up to this point.

↪ Start the video.

Fill-In Observations

↪ There are significantly more fill-ins in this session, but the group should find them helpful in tracking Chip's teaching.

Fill-In Answer Key

1. called	8. truth, love	15. sin
2. sin	9. shared	16. offense
3. primary agent	10. truth	17. unresolved, window
4. personal purity	11. little things	
5. training	12. confession	18. anger
6. honest.	13. angry	19. "I Feel"
7. honesty	14. control	

Transformation Conversation

↪ Depending on your "reading" of the group, you can use one or more of these to get the group started in discussion.

↪ The rest of the questions will allow you to guide the group in discussing the first two training stations. Make sure that the group stays on task in talking about these basic character traits that indicate a person who is experiencing the miracle of life change.

Action Steps

↪ This session includes four Action Steps. Review these and choose two you sense would be most helpful to discuss as a group.

↪ Encourage the group to follow through on each of the Action Steps as a starting point in practicing the training stations.

At Home

↶ As you highlight the assignments, point out that this week will allow them to try out the training station approach. Encourage them to keep track of questions that come up during the following days.

↶ This might be the point to decide whether a wrap-up and review session might be helpful. You may even discuss briefly the idea of scheduling a three- month reunion in order to allow the group to practice some accountability regarding the teaching they have received. Getting that scheduled now will add a new level of seriousness to the application of these principles.

SESSION 10: THE ROLE OF SPIRITUAL TRAINING IN THE LIFE CHANGE PROCESS (2)

Introduction and Video Notes

↶ Welcome and prayer. Consider showing up in a warm-up outfit and commenting that you got so involved in thinking about being in God's Gym that you just had to dress the part. Thank them for their participation and response. The end of the session may be a little rushed.

↶ Consider again whether you need to agree on immediate and/or long-term follow-up sessions.

↶ Start the video.

Fill-In Observations

↶ Once the video session is over, review the fill-ins to make sure people have been able to follow the line of reasoning.

Fill-In Answer Key

1. diligent
2. Financial Stewardship
3. Steal
4. value
5. Good Mentors
6. positive
7. Speech
8. helps
9. unwholesome
10. Positive
11. life, power
12. heart
13. judgment
14. silence, solitude
15. forgiving
16. Private
17. kind
18. Hate
19. attitudes
20. love

Transformation Conversation

➢ Again, the five questions will probably involve more time than is left in the session. Start with number 1 and then give the group permission to decide what other questions they would like to discuss.

Action Steps

➢ Since there is an Action Step related to each of the three training stations in this session, direct the group members to choose one of the exercises and work on it in the next few minutes. The sharing that follows will be varied and give the group a sense of the way God is working in each of their lives.

➢ Save some time to give the group members time to share their responses to the question: Where am I going from here?

➢ After that sharing, close with an extended time of prayer and ask the group members to pray for one another.

At Home

➢ Point out that the At Home assignments will be a practical step into the future. As Chip pointed out in the beginning, this is not a "try harder" scheme. This is a pattern for lifelong spiritual growth. Encourage the group to contact you in the months to come with news of lessons, successes, met goals, and little miracles of life change.

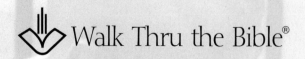
Walk Thru the Bible®

Parenting is a challenge for everyone.

*E*ffective parenting that leads children into a healthy awareness of themselves and God's plan for their lives requires a special commitment, energy, and knowledge that God provides through His Word and teachings that are based on His Word.

Effective Parenting in a Defective World has been designed to give you God's perspective on effectively training your children in the way they should go, as well as provide a sound foundation of hope that renews your energy and commitment to being the best godly parent possible.

You may know of other parents in your church, neighborhood, or school who would benefit from the same knowledge and encouragement to help them more effectively raise their children in a godly way—for both the health of their kids and their own reward.

Share the insights you've gained with them. Let them know how the video has helped you.

You can obtain a gift copy for them by calling ***800-361-6131***, or encouraging them to call for their own copy.

You know that they, too, will reap a huge reward by preparing their kids to deal with the daily issues that the world confronts them with each day. And you will reap the reward of knowing that you helped someone else find a real resource to help meet a real challenge.

Share Your Experience with Another Family.
Call 800-361-6131

Changing the way believers live out their faith...

...by intersecting lives through the application of truth found in God's Word.

Living on the Edge is the broadcast ministry of Walk Thru the Bible featuring the teaching of Chip Ingram. Often dealing with highly relevant and life-impacting issues, Chip's teaching is characterized by strong personal application and scriptural accuracy.

The ministry touches the lives of more than 700,000 people each week, broadcast from radio stations across the United States and in several international markets. To find a station or listen online visit us at www.lote.org.

Hundreds of resources are available in the following areas:

FAMILY & RELATIONSHIPS PERSONAL STRUGGLES KNOWING THE HEART OF GOD LIFE CHANGE

For more information or to order,
contact us at **WWW.LOTE.ORG** or call **888.333.6003**
PLEASE USE CODE MLC0407 WHEN PLACING THIS ORDER

LIVING ON THE EDGE
with Chip Ingram

a ministry of
Walk Thru the Bible

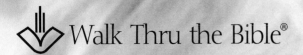